CONTENTS

THE PILLARS OF STRENGTH

A Story of Loss, Responsibility, and Survival

Samuel Okwori

This book is a work of nonfiction. The events, experiences, and reflections presented are presented truthfully from Samuel Okwori's lived experiences and are written and shaped collaboratively with Dr. Rushayne Stewart. Names, places, and events are presented to the best of the authors' knowledge.
This book is intended for educational and reflective purposes. It does not replace professional psychological, medical, legal, or financial advice.

Printed in the United States of America

Dedication

This book is dedicated to my family.
To my father, whose words prepared me even when I did not understand them.
To my mother, whose strength carried us when nothing else could.
To my sisters, for trusting me when I was still learning how to stand.
And to everyone who has had to grow up too soon.
This story is for you.

ACKNOWLEDGMENT

This book exists because of collaboration, trust, and shared commitment to telling the truth with care.

I am deeply grateful to my mother, whose strength and perseverance became my first understanding of endurance, and to my sisters, whose lives gave meaning to every responsibility I carried. Your trust in me shaped the man I continue to become.

I extend my sincere appreciation to Aunty Rose, whose presence during our most painful moments brought stability, comfort, and support when it was needed most. Your role in our lives during loss and transition will always be remembered.

I offer special gratitude to my co-author, **Dr. Rushayne Stewart**. This book was shaped through his writing, guidance, editing, and commitment to bringing my story to life with honesty and dignity. Through many conversations, reflections, and shared moments of vulnerability, he helped translate my lived experiences into words while honoring the truth of my voice. His dedication to this story, both personally and professionally, made this memoir possible.

I am also thankful for the encouragement, belief, and support that came from those who stood with us quietly and consistently. Every word in this book carries traces of that support.

This story is ours to tell, and it is offered with gratitude to everyone who made its telling possible.

INTRODUCTION

Why I Am Telling This Story

My name is Samuel Okwori, and this book is not about having everything figured out. It is about becoming.

I was born and raised in Makurdi, Benue State, Nigeria, in a modest home where responsibility was learned early and survival was often quiet. I am the first son of **Emmanuel Okwori** and **Blessing Okwori**, and the older brother of **Peace Okwori** and **Ihotu Okwori**. We were not a perfect family, but we were bound together by love, duty, and the determination to endure.

Before loss reshaped my life, responsibility was already forming around me. It showed up in small ways, watching, learning, and standing in when needed. At the time, I did not know how much weight those early lessons would eventually carry.

My father was not a perfect man, but he was present. He protected us, cared for us, and never allowed us to starve. He often told me to look after my sisters when he was away. I did not fully understand those words then. I would come to understand them much sooner than I expected.

My mother's strength was quieter but constant. Through her work and perseverance, she showed me that endurance does not always announce itself. Sometimes, it simply continues.

This book is not written to dramatize suffering or to present myself as a hero. It is written to tell the truth about what happens when loss interrupts life, when responsibility arrives without preparation, and when survival becomes a daily practice rather than a choice.

I am telling this story for those who grew up too soon.
For those who carry weight silently.
For those who are still standing, even when the future feels uncertain.

I am not writing from a place of arrival. I am writing from within the journey. There are no perfect endings here, only lessons learned through endurance, presence, and persistence.

Somewhere between loss, responsibility, and survival, I began to understand that strength is not always loud. Often, it is built quietly, over time, by those who refuse to stop moving forward.

My name is Samuel.
Walk with me as I take you through my journey.

The Pillars of Strength: A Story of Loss, Responsibility, and Survival.

CHAPTER ONE

Where I Come From

Makurdi is where my memories live. The town carries a quiet rhythm, mornings that begin slowly, afternoons that stretch under the sun, evenings that soften the edges of the day. Life there taught me patience before it taught me speed. Our home was simple, but it was full. We spoke Idoma and English, not as a choice but as a way of being. Words were how we corrected one another, laughed together, and found comfort when days felt heavy. I learned early that a home is not measured by what it owns but by how it holds its people. Even when things were tight, a sense of togetherness made the space feel larger than it was.

Being the first son placed me in a position of watching and learning. I paid attention to how my parents carried responsibility, how they made decisions quietly, and how they protected what mattered without announcing it. My father's presence was steady. He believed in order, care, and doing what needed to be done. He didn't speak much about strength, but he lived it in small, consistent ways. My mother's strength moved differently. It showed up in persistence, early mornings, long days, and tired hands that still found a way to keep going. She didn't complain; she endured.

I grew up understanding that effort was normal. Nothing was handed to us easily, and that reality shaped my expectations of life before I even understood them. Our home taught me discipline without harshness. Correction came with care, and expectations were wrapped in love. Even mistakes became lessons rather than punishments. There were moments of joy that didn't require money, shared meals, quiet laughter, and conversations that lingered into the evening. Those moments anchored me more than I realized at the time. School became important early on. Education was spoken of as a doorway, a chance to see beyond the limits of our immediate surroundings. I held onto that idea, even when it felt distant.

I learned to value effort over outcome. Trying mattered. Showing up mattered. These lessons settled into me long before life tested them. Looking back now, I see how these early years shaped my sense of responsibility. Not as a burden, but as an awareness, an understanding that my actions mattered beyond myself. Makurdi gave me more than a place to grow up. It gave me grounding. It taught me how to stand quietly and observe before speaking or acting. Those beginnings did not promise an easy future, but they gave me something just as important: a foundation strong enough to carry weight.

Before loss entered my story, before responsibility demanded more of me, this was where I learned what it meant to belong.

Responsibility Forming Quietly

Responsibility did not arrive in my life with a clear announcement. It crept in quietly, shaped by observation rather than instruction. Long before anyone called me strong, I was learning how to carry myself in ways that mattered. As the firstborn, I felt an unspoken awareness that my every move was being watched. Not watched in fear, but in expectation. I understood that what I did set an example, even when no one said it out loud. My father rarely sat me down to explain responsibility. Instead, he showed it through consistency. He handled problems without drama, protected his family without hesitation, and made sure what needed to be done was done.

There were moments when he would remind me to look after my sisters, especially when he was not around. At the time, it sounded like advice meant for small moments. I didn't know it was shaping my identity. My mother reinforced responsibility in her own way. She trusted me with small tasks, simple errands, and quiet expectations. Those moments taught me that responsibility grows when it is trusted, not forced.

I learned early that being dependable mattered. Showing up, even when tired, mattered. Finishing what I started mattered. These lessons settled into me without resistance. There were days I wanted to act like a child, to avoid thinking too far ahead. But responsibility has a way of pulling you forward gently, reminding you that others depend on you in ways you cannot ignore. I noticed how my parents made sacrifices without naming them. They gave up comfort, rest, and sometimes their own needs to ensure the family remained stable. Watching that shaped how I understood love.

Responsibility began to feel less like a burden and more like a role I was slowly stepping into. It was not heavy yet, but it was present, waiting. In school and at home, I learned to manage myself. I learned restraint, patience, and the value of thinking before acting. These habits formed quietly, without applause. There was no pressure to be perfect, but there was an expectation to be mindful. I carried that expectation with me, even when I didn't fully understand its purpose. As I grew older, responsibility became part of how I saw myself. It influenced my decisions, my posture, and the way I interacted with others. I didn't know then how much that early training would matter. I only knew that I was becoming someone others could rely on, even in small ways.

My father had a special tenderness for my youngest sister. As the last born, she was spoiled in a way only love allows pampered, protected, and surrounded by his attention. He laughed more easily with her, carried her longer, and made sure she never felt forgotten. Watching him love her that way taught me something I did not yet have words for. He showed me that strength could be gentle, that responsibility could be rooted in care, and that protection did not always come from authority, but from affection. After he died, that love did not disappear. It settled into me, quietly shaping how I felt toward her and the role I would one day have to carry. Those early years were shaping me for a future I could not yet imagine. They were preparing me to carry a weight I had not yet been asked to lift.

Before loss demanded more of me, responsibility had already taken root. Quietly, steadily, it was becoming part of who I was.

CHAPTER TWO

The Day Everything Changed

The day my father died did not announce itself with thunder. It arrived quietly, like a wrong turn taken without realizing it. I remember ordinary sounds, the kind that usually fade into the background, suddenly becoming sharp and unforgettable. There was confusion before there was clarity. Conversations happened around me, but they felt distant, as if they were taking place in another room. I was present, yet separated from everything unfolding in front of me. Time behaved strangely that day. Minutes stretched and collapsed at the same time. Waiting became unbearable, not because of what I knew, but because of what I feared I was about to learn.

We took my father to one hospital, then another. Each place felt the same; questions without answers, waiting without progress. By the time we were on our way to a third hospital, he was growing weaker, and I pulled him close so he could rest. His head lay on my lap while I held his hand, trying to believe that getting there would change something. His grip was faint, unfamiliar, frightening. As we moved, his hand went still. I did not understand it immediately. I kept holding him, waiting for movement, waiting for breath. Then it became clear. My father died with his head in my lap. In that moment, I felt weak in a way I had never known, confused, unprepared. It was the first time I had watched someone so close to me leave this world, right in front of me, while I was holding him, and there was nothing I could do to stop it.

When the truth settled in, it didn't come with immediate tears. It came with a stillness that felt heavier than crying. My body reacted before my mind could catch up. I thought of my father as someone who always returned home. No matter how late or tired he was, he came back. The idea that he would not walk through the door again felt impossible to accept. The house felt different almost instantly. The walls seemed closer, the air thicker. Even familiar spaces felt unfamiliar, as though something essential had been removed. I remember standing still, unsure of what to do with my hands, my thoughts, my breath. Grief does not always rush in; it sometimes waits, watching to see how you will respond. My mother's strength faltered in a way I had never seen before. Her silence spoke louder than any cry. In that moment, I realized that something deeper than loss had entered our lives. People came and went, offering words that floated past me without landing. Comfort felt abstract, distant. Nothing anyone said could reach where the pain had settled.

I wanted to understand what had happened, but understanding felt useless. Knowing the details did not soften the reality. It only made it permanent. I thought about my sisters, even before I fully thought about myself. Their faces came to mind, and with them, a fear I could not yet name. Something had shifted, and I could feel it pressing toward me. Grief began to take shape as responsibility loomed quietly behind it. I didn't know what that meant yet, but I sensed that life was preparing to ask more of me than I felt ready to give. There is a moment when loss moves from being news to becoming truth.

That moment found me standing in a place I did not recognize, inside a life I could not yet understand. Nothing on that day prepared me for what came after. It only marked the end of what had been. The certainty I had lived with was gone. That was the day everything changed, not loudly, not dramatically, but completely. I did not yet know what would be required of me, only that life had already begun to ask.

Becoming The Man Of The House

Grief did not give us time to sit still. Almost immediately, life began asking questions that had no easy answers. Decisions needed to be made, arrangements discussed, and roles quietly reassigned. I noticed the shift in how people looked at me. Conversations that once passed over my head now paused in front of me. Expectations formed without being spoken, and I felt them settling on my shoulders. My mother needed support in ways I had never been asked to give before. Her strength was still there, but it leaned differently. I became aware that my presence now mattered in a new way. My sisters stayed close, their silence louder than their words. I could see uncertainty in their eyes, and with it came a responsibility I could not ignore. They needed reassurance, even when I did not feel reassured myself. There was no ceremony to mark the change. No one officially told me I was now the man of the house.

It happened naturally, through necessity, through absence, through the sudden weight of being needed.

I began thinking ahead in ways I hadn't before. Simple questions turned heavy. What comes next? How do we manage? What happens if I fail? These thoughts crowded my mind without pause. Grief and responsibility overlapped in uncomfortable ways. I wanted space to mourn, but life kept pulling me forward. There was no pause button, no moment to catch my breath.

One thing my family held onto firmly during that time was prayer. We took it seriously, not as a ritual, but as a lifeline. In the days after my father's death, prayer became one of the few places where our pain could exist without explanation. Sometimes we prayed aloud, sometimes in silence. It did not erase the grief or lighten the responsibility I was carrying, but it steadied me. Prayer became the beginning of my healing, not because it fixed everything, but because it gave me somewhere to place the weight I could no longer carry alone.

I learned quickly that strength is not always confidence. Sometimes it is silence. Sometimes it is standing even when your legs feel weak. I did what needed to be done because there was no alternative. Fear followed me closely during that time. Fear of making mistakes. Fear of not being enough. Fear of letting my family down when they needed stability the most.

I tried to hide that fear, believing that showing it would make things worse. I thought being strong meant being unshaken. I didn't yet understand that strength often exists alongside fear. Responsibility reshaped how I saw myself. I was no longer just a son or a student. I was becoming a protector, a decision-maker, someone others depended on.

My father did not leave us wealth or detailed instructions for the future, but he left a legacy that mattered just as much. He lived with kindness, worked hard without complaint, and loved deeply. Those values shaped our home long before his absence did. After his death, I understood that legacy is not something you inherit, it is something you choose to carry forward. I did not feel called to replace him, but I felt responsible to honor what he stood for. As I stepped into new responsibilities, I tried to live with the same kindness, the same work ethic, and the same love, while still finding my own path in life. His life became something I would live from, not live under.

There were moments when I felt overwhelmed by the weight of it all. The expectations were heavy, and the path ahead was unclear. Still, stopping was never an option. I began to measure my choices differently. Every action felt connected to someone else's well-being. That awareness changed how I moved through each day. I did not feel ready for the role I had stepped into. But readiness did not matter. Responsibility had arrived, and it demanded presence, not perfection. That was how I became the man of the house, not through age or preparation, but through necessity. Grief had opened the door, and responsibility walked in and stayed.

Loss does not ask if you are ready. It enters, rearranges everything, and leaves you standing in a life you did not choose. What followed my father's death was not only grief, but the sudden awareness that responsibility does not wait for healing. Certainty disappeared, and in its place came weight, unfamiliar, heavy, and unavoidable. Strength was no longer something to grow into overtime; it became a requirement overnight. I did not yet know how I would manage what came next. I only knew that standing still was no longer an option.

CHAPTER THREE

Hunger Has a Voice

Hunger entered our lives quietly, without warning. It did not arrive all at once; it crept in, one missed meal at a time, until it became part of our daily reality. At first, we tried to manage with what we had. Small portions were stretched, meals were delayed, and excuses were made. We told ourselves it was temporary, that things would improve soon. But days passed, and improvement did not come. The space between meals grew wider, and the uncertainty became harder to ignore. Hunger settled in like an unwelcome guest that refused to leave. There were mornings when I woke up already tired, not from lack of sleep, but from the weight of knowing there was nothing to eat. My body felt lighter, but my thoughts felt heavier.

Garri became more than food; it became survival. Sometimes it was mixed with water, sometimes taken dry. Other times, there was only water. We learned how to quell hunger instead of satisfying it. The hardest part was pretending everything was normal. Outside our home, life continued as usual. Inside, we learned how to live with less than what was needed. I watched my mother make decisions no parent should have to make. She measured food carefully, ensuring my sisters ate first. I learned to accept less without complaint.

There were nights when hunger kept me awake. My stomach ached, but my thoughts ached more. I worried about tomorrow, about how long this could last, about what would happen if nothing changed. Poverty has a way of shrinking your world. Simple things begin to feel unreachable. Needs turn into wishes, and wishes turn into silence. I felt the shame of not being able to provide, even when I was doing everything I could. Being responsible did not always mean being capable, and that truth was painful to accept.

There were moments when I questioned myself. Was I failing? Was I doing enough? Hunger has a way of turning doubt inward, making you your own harshest critic. Despite everything, I learned how to endure. Hunger forced me to become aware of what mattered most. It stripped life down to essentials, leaving no room for illusion. I began to understand that survival is not dramatic. It is repetitive, exhausting, and often unseen. It is choosing to keep going even when your body asks for rest.

Food was scarce, but determination prevailed. Even in hunger, I refused to surrender to hopelessness. Something in me insisted that this could not be the end of the story. Hunger found its voice in our home, but it did not take our will. It changed us, tested us, and revealed our limits, but it also prepared me for the strength I would soon need to find.

Depression, Anxiety, And Carrying Too Much

Poverty did not only empty our plates; it began to empty me from the inside. The hunger I felt in my body slowly found its way into my thoughts, my emotions, and the way I saw myself. Some mornings, I woke up heavy, even before anything had happened. My chest felt tight, my mind restless. I carried a sadness I could not explain and an anxiety that followed me through the day. I started worrying constantly about food, about school, about my sisters, about my mother. The questions never stopped. What if this gets worse? What if I fail them? What if I am not enough?

Grief had not finished its work in me. Losing my father left a space that could not be filled, and poverty pressed into that space, making it harder to breathe. I was grieving and surviving at the same time, and neither gave me rest. There were days when I felt overwhelmed by everything I was carrying. I felt older than my age, tired beyond sleep, and stretched thin by responsibilities I had not chosen.

I learned how to hide what I was feeling. I smiled when I needed to. I spoke when I had to. But inside, I was struggling to hold myself together. Being the strong one left little room for weakness. Anxiety made small problems feel enormous. A simple delay could send my thoughts racing. Silence felt dangerous. Waiting felt unbearable. My mind was always preparing for the next thing to go wrong. There were moments when I questioned my worth. Poverty has a way of making you feel invisible, as if your efforts do not matter because the results are not immediate. That feeling settled deep inside me.

I felt guilty for feeling weak. I told myself I had no right to be tired, no right to feel low when others depended on me. That guilt kept me moving, even when I needed rest. At times, sadness came without warning. It would sit with me quietly, heavy and uninvited. I did not always have the words for it, but I knew something inside me was hurting.

What kept me from giving up completely were the people around me. My mother's resilience, my sisters' presence, and the responsibility I carried for them anchored me when my thoughts drifted too far. I also held onto the belief that this season was not permanent. Even when I could not see change, I believed it was possible. That belief was fragile, but it was enough to keep me standing.

I learned that depression and anxiety do not always look dramatic. Sometimes they look like endurance. Sometimes they look like silence. Sometimes they look like continuing when you want to stop. There are still days when sadness returns, and anxiety whispers doubt. Those feelings did not disappear overnight. But they no longer define me the way they once did.

I am still holding onto hope, not as something loud or guaranteed, but as something steady. Even as I struggle, I choose to believe that survival can lead to change, and that this weight will not always be mine to carry. Hunger and emotional exhaustion revealed parts of me I did not know existed. They stripped away comfort and illusion, leaving only endurance. Survival became less about tomorrow and more about making it through the day.

There was no space for pretending. Loss and poverty demanded honesty, about fear, about weakness, about how heavy life had become. Strength did not feel heroic; it felt necessary.

What I carried forward was not clarity or answers, but awareness. And that awareness would shape how I moved through everything that followed.

When The Weight Almost Broke Me

There were moments when everything I carried felt too heavy to hold. On those days, I shut down. I would go into my room, turn off my phone, and disconnect from everyone. No talking. No explanations. Just me alone with my thoughts, trying to quiet a mind that refused to rest.

The pressure followed me even in silence. I worried constantly about how I would pay my sisters' school fees, how I would put food on the table, how I would support my mother when she needed something I could not yet provide. I wanted to start a small business, to create a way forward, but money remained the barrier. Every idea stopped where resources ended.

There were times when depression felt close enough to pull me under. Moments when I cried until there were no tears left. Moments when giving up felt easier than continuing. I did not want to disappear, but I was exhausted from holding everything together.

Sometimes my mother would tell me she needed something, money for food, school, or the house, and seeing her cry would break my heart. I wanted to help her. I wanted to be enough. But wanting did not always translate into ability, and that gap felt unbearable.

I dreamed of improving our home, adding a fence, installing outside lights so my family could feel safer. But even those small plans felt unreachable. Each delay reminded me of what I could not yet afford.

Watching my peers move forward made it harder. People my age were building lives without the weight I carried. I found myself asking questions I could not answer. Why did my father have to die now? Why did he have to go when we needed him most? In the middle of those moments, God often sent someone to interrupt my despair. Many times, that person was Rushayne.

Sometimes it was a simple message, a joke that made me pause. Other times it was a phone call where he did not rush me or try to fix everything. He listened. I talked about my fears, my stress, my frustration. Often, all I needed was to be heard. And sometimes, during or after those conversations, I would receive a notification. A small deposit. It was never much, but it was enough; enough to buy food, enough to handle something urgent, enough to breathe. In those moments, I would break down and cry. Not just because of the money, but because someone saw me.

In October 2025, I finally met Rushayne in person when he visited Nigeria. He invited me to Lagos and paid for my airfare. I stayed with him for a week. We went out, visited parks, ate together, and spent time around places like the convention center near Lekki. For the first time in a long while, I felt light.

A week later, he traveled to Benue to meet my family. My mother welcomed him warmly. He called her "Mama," and she called him "my son." She cooked for him, and we spent time together as a family. He taught us games, dominoes, cards, and drafts, as we laughed in ways that felt unfamiliar but healing. We ate vegetable soup and fufu, went out to a restaurant, attended church, and shared moments of simple joy.

When it was time for him to return to Lagos and then to New York City, it was hard to say goodbye. But something had shifted. The weight was still there, but I was no longer carrying it alone. I was still struggling. Still not financially stable. Still learning. But I had been reminded that even in the hardest seasons, God can send help, not always to remove the burden, but to help you survive it.

Survival does not always look the way we imagine it will. Sometimes it is not bravery or bold decisions, but endurance, quiet, uncelebrated, and unseen. There were no clear victories during this season, only days that ended and mornings that began again. What I carried was not just hunger or responsibility, but the weight of uncertainty. Not knowing how things would turn out became part of my daily reality. And yet, I learned that continuing without answers is still a form of strength.

There were moments when hope felt distant, fragile, almost unnecessary. But even then, something within me refused to completely let go. Not because I was strong, but because stopping felt more frightening than continuing.

This chapter of my life did not teach me how to escape hardship. It taught me how to stay present inside it. How to keep breathing when the weight did not lift. How to survive without applause. I did not emerge from this season healed or finished. I emerged aware, aware of my limits, my fears, and the quiet ways help can arrive. Awareness became the bridge between endurance and change.

What followed was not immediate relief, but something subtler. A pause. A moment to gather what remained of myself before moving forward.

A Quiet Reflection

If you've made it this far, you've already carried a lot with these pages.

You've walked through beginnings shaped by responsibility, through loss that came without warning, and through survival that demanded more than anyone should have to give. None of it has been loud or dramatic. It has been steady, heavy, and real.

This is the part of the story many people live, but rarely pause to acknowledge. The part where you keep going because stopping isn't an option. The part where strength looks like endurance, and hope feels small but necessary.

I won't promise that what comes next is easy. But I will tell you this: the story does not rest in what was lost. Survival has a way of revealing what is still possible, even when the path forward isn't clear yet.

If any of this feels familiar, you are not alone. And if you're wondering whether to keep turning the page, I invite you to stay. There is more to this journey than what has already been carried.

Sometimes, the most important part of a story begins right after the weight feels heaviest.

CHAPTER FOUR

Using My Voice to Survive

Survival eventually pushed me toward action. Sitting with pain and uncertainty could only take me so far before I needed to do something, anything that might change our situation, even slightly. I had always been comfortable speaking. Words came naturally to me, and I knew how to hold attention when given the chance. Still, turning that ability into something practical felt risky. Trying and failing felt more dangerous than staying still. The idea of hosting events didn't come from confidence; it came from necessity. I needed a way to contribute, a way to bring something home when nothing else seemed available. My first opportunities were small. Weddings, gatherings, and modest events where expectations were low, but pressure felt high. Each time I stood in front of people, I carried more than a microphone; I carried responsibility. I learned quickly that talent alone was not enough. Preparation mattered. Presence mattered. I had to show up ready, even when everything inside me felt uncertain.

There was no steady income. Some weeks brought opportunity, others brought silence. If there were no events, there would be no money. That reality made every booking feel urgent. I began measuring time differently. Days were no longer about comfort or rest; they were about possibility. Could something come through today? Would this effort make a difference?

Standing before a crowd demanded focus. For a few hours, I could set aside the weight I carried and concentrate on the moment. In those moments, my voice gave me distance from everything pressing on my mind. Still, fear followed me closely. Fear of being overlooked. Fear of not being good enough. Fear that this effort would not be enough to change anything.

Each event taught me something new. How to read a room. How to adjust. How to remain calm when things didn't go as planned. These lessons built confidence slowly, without promise. I realized that survival often begins with using what you already have. I did not wait for perfect conditions or full certainty. I used my voice because it was available to me. There were days when exhaustion made it hard to keep trying. But giving up felt heavier than continuing. Responsibility demanded persistence, even when results were inconsistent.

Hosting events did not solve everything. It did not erase hunger or fear. But it created movement where there had been stagnation. Through this process, I began to see myself differently. Not just as someone enduring life, but as someone participating in it actively, intentionally.

Becoming an event host (MC) was not about recognition or applause. It was about survival. It was about taking one step forward when standing still was no longer an option.

My voice became more than sound. It became a tool, one

of the first ways I learned that even in struggle, I still had something to offer.

Speaking To Stay Alive

There were days when speaking was the only thing that kept me from sinking too far into my thoughts. Silence had its place, but too much of it left room for fear to grow unchecked.

When I wasn't hosting events, my mind often returned to the same worries. Money. School. Home. The future. These thoughts followed me closely, especially on days when nothing seemed to move forward.

I discovered that expressing myself created space inside me. Speaking allowed me to release what I could not always explain. It gave shape to emotions that otherwise stayed tangled.

That need to express myself led me online. At first, it wasn't about being seen or heard by many; it was about distraction. It was about staying mentally present when my reality felt overwhelming.

Going live became a way to stay connected. I spoke, shared, and engaged without fully revealing everything I was carrying. In those moments, my voice helped me feel less alone.

I learned that not everything I faced needed to be shared. Some struggles were mine to carry quietly. I began to understand that silence can be protective, not empty.

There were people who listened with genuine interest, and others who were simply curious. Over time, I learned to tell the difference. That awareness helped me guard my peace.

Speaking became a form of balance. It allowed me to release pressure without exposing my wounds completely. I could be present without being vulnerable to everyone.

There were moments when sadness still found me mid-sentence. I learned how to pause, breathe, and continue. Those pauses taught me that strength does not always require pushing through; it sometimes requires slowing down.

My voice helped me remain emotionally alive. Even on difficult days, it gave me a sense of purpose, a reason to engage with the world beyond my struggles.

I realized that expression doesn't always bring answers, but it brings relief. Speaking helped me organize my thoughts and regain a sense of control.

Over time, I grew more comfortable with who I was becoming. Not fearless, but aware. Not fixed, but moving forward. My voice reflected that growth.

I stopped measuring my worth by how much I shared or how much I hid. Instead, I focused on honesty with myself and intention in how I spoke.

Using my voice this way did not erase my struggles. But it kept me from being consumed by them. It gave me a way to stay grounded when everything felt uncertain.

Speaking became a form of survival, not because it changed my circumstances immediately, but because it reminded me that I was still here, still thinking, still moving.

In finding my voice, I found something just as important: the ability to choose when to speak and when to remain silent. That choice gave me strength I didn't know I had.

Finding my voice did not change my circumstances, but it

created movement. It gave me a way to participate in my own survival rather than simply endure it.

Using what I had imperfectly and without certainty opened space for possibility. Speaking became a way to stay present when everything else felt unstable.

My voice did not rescue me from struggle. But it reminded me that I still had something to offer, and that knowledge mattered more than I understood at the time.

CHAPTER FIVE

Help That Found Me While I Was Still Struggling

The Ones Who Stayed

Grief can make a home feel empty even when people are present. After my father died, our house was full of silence, questions, and exhaustion. In the middle of that heaviness, Aunty Rose showed up. She did not come with long speeches or perfect words. She came with presence. She sat with us, listened, and allowed our pain to exist without trying to rush it away.

My mother received her not just as a friend, but as a big sister. There was comfort in that bond, something steady in a moment when everything felt unstable. Aunty Rose became a quiet support my mother could lean on. When the reality of burial arrangements set in, the weight grew heavier. Decisions had to be made while grief was still raw. Aunty Rose stepped in without hesitation, helping in ways that mattered when energy and strength were low.

She drove her car from Benue to my father's village in **Otukpo Atrukpo**, staying present through the journey and the moments that followed. That act alone spoke louder than words. Being there for the burial was not easy. Emotions were exposed, and final goodbyes carried a weight that could not be shared lightly. Aunty Rose stayed through it all, steady and supportive.

What mattered most was that her support did not end when the burial ended. Many people fade away once ceremonies are over, but she remained present, checking in and standing with my mother and us. She understood that grief does not follow a schedule. Some days were harder than others, and her consistency reminded us that we were not facing everything alone.

There were moments when her presence gave my mother space to breathe. In those moments, I saw how support can restore strength quietly, without needing recognition. As time passed, life continued to demand effort. School, responsibility, and survival pressed forward. Aunty Rose remained part of that journey, not as someone solving problems, but as someone standing nearby.

On **December 4, 2025**, my final day of school arrived. It was a moment my father could not witness. Aunty Rose was there. Her presence that day felt like a bridge between what was lost and what was still possible. Seeing her there reminded me that support does not always come from where you expect it. Sometimes, it comes from those who choose to stay when it would be easier to leave.

Her role in our lives taught me something important. Survival is not always about strength alone; it is about community, about people who step in when you are stretched thin. Aunty Rose did not replace what we lost. No one could. But she helped steady us while we found our footing again. In a season marked by loss and uncertainty, her presence became one of the quiet ways we learned that survival does not have to be carried alone.

Encouragement That Kept Me Going

Help did not come into my life all at once. It arrived slowly, through conversation, consistency, and someone choosing to care even as they carried their own weight. That person was **Dr. Rushayne Stewart**. We connected while I was trying to stay afloat. There was no promise made, no grand speech about changing my life. What stood out first was attention, being seen without being interrogated, heard without being rushed. As I learned more about him, I realized he was not speaking from comfort. He had faced cancer. He had lost his mother to cancer. He was navigating his own seasons of uncertainty. Yet, he still made space to show up for someone else.

That mattered to me. It showed me that strength is not the absence of struggle, but the decision to keep caring anyway. His life became proof that pain does not disqualify you from helping others. Sometimes the support came as encouragement, words that reminded me not to give up when everything felt heavy. Other times, it came in practical ways, small but timely, helping me keep moving forward when I was close to stopping. What stayed with me most was consistency. Even when he was not working, even when his own life was demanding, he remained present. That presence reminded me that help does not need to be perfect to be powerful.

He shared something with me that reshaped how I understood strength. He would say, *"Silent rivers run deep."* And then he explained it in a way that stayed with me.

> *"Silent rivers run deep.*

> *Not because a person is silent doesn't mean there is nothing to say.*
> *Often, silence is the best defense and the best response.*
> *Silence keeps them guessing.*
> *Silence keeps them wondering." And one day at a time."*

I began to understand that not every struggle needs to be explained. Not every burden needs an audience. Some people are not concerned about what you are carrying; they are only curious about your business. I understood that in taking life one day at a time as it comes, I can overcome it slowly while remaining strong. That realization changed how I moved. I learned to guard my peace. I learned that silence can be strength, not weakness. It can be protection, not avoidance.

His example also showed me what persistence looks like. Even as he faced loss and uncertainty, he continued writing, creating, and believing that purpose does not end when circumstances are difficult. Watching that inspired me. It reminded me that I did not need to wait for life to be perfect before continuing. Progress could happen alongside struggle.

There were moments when doubt returned, when the weight felt too heavy again. In those moments, encouragement mattered more than answers. Knowing someone believed in me helped me believe in myself. Support like that does not erase pain. It does not remove responsibility. But it makes carrying the load feel possible. I learned that survival is not always about what you do alone. Sometimes it is about who reminds you that you are not alone, even when the road is long.

Encouragement kept me going when exhaustion told me to stop. It helped me stay focused when distractions felt easier to resist. Through shared pain and steady presence, I learned that help could come from people who are still fighting their own battles, and that kind of help carries a strength on its own.

Looking back, I see that help did not arrive in one dramatic moment. It came through people who stayed. Some stood with us in grief. Others spoke into my life when my mind felt heavy. None of them removed my responsibility, but they reminded me that I was not carrying it alone.

This chapter taught me that survival is not always about rescue. Sometimes it is about presence. Sometimes it is about someone listening, encouraging, or simply showing up when life feels unbearable. That kind of help does not erase pain, but it makes endurance possible.

What I carried after this chapter, I carried differently. Not because the weight disappeared, but because I understood that strength can be shared. Quietly. Faithfully. Without needing to be seen.

CHAPTER SIX

Still Standing

Graduation did not feel like an ending. It felt more like a pause, a moment to acknowledge distance traveled without pretending the journey was complete. I stood at that point aware that survival had brought me far, but not all the way. Finishing school carried quiet relief. There was no celebration large enough to announce it, no sense that life had suddenly shifted. Responsibility still waited, unchanged, asking for the same commitment it had always asked for.

I thought about how much effort it took to reach that moment. The late nights, the pressure, the hunger, the anxiety, the emotional weight. None of them disappeared simply because a requirement had been met. There were expectations from others, and expectations I placed on myself. Graduation was supposed to feel triumphant. Instead, it felt honest. I had completed something important, even if the road ahead remained uncertain.

I learned that progress does not always feel satisfying when survival is still ongoing. Achievement and struggle can exist in the same space, without canceling each other out. Responsibility did not loosen its grip. My family still needed me. Life still demanded consistency. The title of graduate did not erase the realities waiting outside the ceremony. There were moments when I questioned whether finishing was enough. Whether effort without immediate reward still counted. Those questions lingered, unanswered but present.

I realized that endurance teaches patience in ways comfort never could. It reshapes how you measure success, forcing you to value persistence over applause. Standing at that point, I did not feel complete. I felt aware. Aware of how far I had come, and aware of how much farther there was to go. There was a quiet pride in knowing I did not stop. Not because it was easy, but because stopping was never an option. That mattered more than recognition.

I learned that arriving is not always a destination you reach. Sometimes it is a mindset you develop, a willingness to keep moving forward even when certainty is absent. Life after finishing required the same discipline as life before it. The same focus. The same resolve. Survival does not end when milestones are crossed. What changed was not my circumstances, but my perspective. I had evidence now that endurance could carry me through demanding seasons. I did not celebrate loudly. I reflected quietly. I allowed myself to acknowledge effort without demanding immediate transformation.

Finishing without arriving taught me something essential: survival is not about where you end up. It is about refusing to stop, even when the road continues beyond what you can see.

Choosing To Keep Going

Life did not slow down after finishing school. If anything, it continued with the same urgency it always had. Responsibilities remained, questions remained, and the future still felt open and uncertain. Some days felt heavier than others. There were moments when sadness returned without warning, when anxiety reminded me of everything that still needed attention. Those feelings did not mean failure; they meant I was human.

I learned that choosing to keep going is not a one-time decision. It is something you do daily, sometimes hourly, especially when progress feels slow and effort feels invisible. Hope did not arrive loudly. It did not erase struggle or guarantee outcomes. It showed up quietly, as a decision to believe that change was possible even when evidence was limited. I stopped waiting for life to become easier before moving forward. Instead, I learned how to move while carrying weight, adjusting my pace without abandoning direction.

Responsibility no longer felt like punishment. It felt like a purpose. Caring for others, showing up consistently, and remaining dependable became part of how I defined strength. There were lessons in patience I could not have learned any other way. Endurance taught me how to stand when nothing around me felt stable. I became more intentional about what I shared and what I kept to myself. Protecting my peace became just as important as pursuing progress. Silence, when chosen wisely, became strength.

I learned to measure success differently. Not by comparison, but by consistency. Not by applause, but by effort. Not by perfection, but by persistence. There were moments when doubt returned, asking if the road ahead was worth continuing. Each time, I answered by taking the next step anyway. Choosing to keep going did not mean ignoring fear. It meant moving forward despite it. Courage was not the absence of uncertainty; it was action in the presence of it.

I stopped waiting for the arrival. I accepted that becoming is ongoing, and that growth often happens quietly, without witnesses. Strength no longer meant carrying everything alone. It meant knowing when to pause, when to speak, and when to remain silent. I am still standing, not because life has been gentle, but because I have learned how to remain present within it. Survival shaped me, responsibility grounded me, and endurance carried me forward.

This journey is not finished. But I am no longer afraid of what lies ahead. I choose to keep going, steady, aware, and committed to whatever comes next.

CONCLUSION

This story does not end with everything resolved. It ends with understanding.

When I look back on the journey behind these pages, I no longer see strength as a single moment or a personal achievement. What held me up was not one decision or one breakthrough, but many pillars formed slowly over time, often without my awareness.

One pillar was loss. Grief entered my life suddenly and stayed longer than I expected. Losing my father reshaped everything I thought I knew about stability, safety, and certainty. Loss weakened me in ways I did not anticipate, but it also deepened me. It taught me that strength can grow from pain, even when pain is never chosen.

Another pillar was responsibility. Being needed forced me to stand when I wanted to sit, to decide when I wanted to rest, and to carry weight before I felt ready. Responsibility did not make life easier, but it gave my days direction when clarity was absent. It disciplined me, shaped my character, and taught me that showing up matters, even when confidence is missing.

Survival became its own pillar. It was built through hunger, endurance, and repetition, through waking up and trying again when nothing felt certain. Survival taught me patience and humility. It showed me that continuing, even without visible progress, is still movement. Sometimes, surviving the day is enough.

There were quieter pillars too. Prayer became a place where pain could exist without explanation, where healing could begin without pressure. Presence mattered, people who stayed, who listened, who did not rush my grief or minimize my struggle. Encouragement arrived in unexpected ways. Silence became a form of protection. These pillars were not always visible, but they were strong enough to hold me when I felt close to breaking.

Legacy also became a pillar. My father did not leave wealth behind, but he left values, kindness, hard work, and love. Honoring that legacy did not mean replacing him or becoming someone I was not. It meant carrying forward what mattered, while still finding my own path in life. Together, these pillars became my strength. Not a strength that demands attention or announces itself loudly, but one that holds steady under pressure. A strength that allows breaking and rebuilding. A strength that understands becoming takes time.

I am still becoming. Still learning. Still standing. These pillars are not finished structures; they are living supports, reinforced each time I choose to keep going despite uncertainty. If there is meaning to be found here, it is this: strength is rarely a single moment. It is a structure built slowly, often invisibly, by those who refuse to give up even when the future is unclear.

This is not the end of the journey. It is simply the place where I pause long enough to recognize what has been holding me up all along.

PERSONAL MESSAGE TO THE READER

Dear Reader,

If you are reading this, I want you to know something important: I am not writing from a place of arrival. I am writing from a place of becoming, a place of finding strength in my pain. I am still struggling. I am still learning. I am still working toward stability. There are days when the weight feels heavy again, and nights when questions return. Life did not suddenly become easy because I finished this book. But I am still here, and maybe you are too.

If you are reading this while feeling tired, overwhelmed, forgotten, or unseen, I want you to know that your life still has value, even in this moment. Especially in this moment. Survival does not mean you are weak. It means you are enduring something that would have broken others. There were times in my life when I had nothing but responsibility and hope that felt too small to trust. There were moments when I questioned whether my effort mattered, whether continuing made sense. What kept me going was not certainty; it was the belief that my story was not finished, even when it felt unfinished.

If you are in a season where you feel stuck, hungry, grieving, or afraid of what tomorrow holds, please hear this: your current struggle is not your final definition. You may not see the change yet, but survival itself is evidence that something in you refuses to give up. I am not writing to tell you that everything will suddenly work out. I am writing to tell you that you are allowed to keep going even when things are not working out yet. You are allowed to hope quietly. You are allowed to move slowly. You are allowed to believe that becoming takes time.

If my story has done anything, I hope it has reminded you that strength does not always roar. Sometimes it whispers, *"Try again tomorrow."*

And if today is all you can manage, that is enough. ***"Healing cannot start where pain is denied."*** -Dr. Rushayne Stewart

I am still walking this road. And if you are too, know that you are not walking it alone.

Warm regards,

Samuel Okwori

A NOTE ON ENCOURAGEMENT AND RESILIENCE

This book was never written to suggest that life suddenly becomes easy.

It was written to be honest.

There are still days when the struggle feels heavy. There are still unanswered questions, unfinished goals, and moments when the future feels uncertain. Healing is not a straight path, and resilience does not mean the absence of pain. It means choosing to continue, even when progress feels slow or invisible.

There were seasons in this story where survival looked like silence, where strength meant getting through the day, and where hope felt fragile. If you find yourself in a similar place, know this: struggling does not mean you are failing. It means you are human.

Faith, support, and encouragement did not remove the weight I carried, but they helped me hold it. Sometimes resilience is built through prayer. Sometimes it is strengthened by someone who listens. Sometimes it grows simply because you refused to give up, even when you were tired of being strong.

If you are reading this while facing your own challenges, do not measure your life by what you have not yet reached.

Growth often happens quietly, long before it becomes visible. Becoming takes time.

Let this book remind you of something simple, but important:

- ✓ You are allowed to keep going, even when you are exhausted.
- ✓ You are allowed to rest without quitting.
- ✓ You are allowed to hope, even when certainty is missing.

Resilience is not loud. It does not demand attention. But it lasts.

ABOUT THE AUTHOR

Samuel Okwori

Samuel Okwori was born and raised in Makurdi, Benue State, Nigeria. He is the firstborn in his family and a graduate with a bachelor's degree in English Language and Literature from Benue State University.

After the sudden loss of his father while still a university student, Samuel was forced to grow up quickly, taking on responsibility for his family while navigating grief, poverty, and emotional struggle. His journey has been shaped by endurance, quiet resilience, and the determination to keep going even when life felt unfinished. Samuel is not writing from a place of arrival, but from a place of becoming. The Pillars of Strength is his first memoir, written to give voice to those who carry weight silently and to remind readers that survival itself is meaningful.

ABOUT THE AUTHOR

Dr. Rushayne Stewart - Co-Author

Dr. Rushayne Stewart is a writer, life coach, Christian counselor, Philanthropist, and mentor whose work centers on storytelling, resilience, and the human capacity to endure hardship with dignity. He has authored multiple books focused on faith, psychology, grief, and personal transformation.

As co-author, Dr. Stewart worked closely with Samuel Okwori to shape, write, edit, and bring this memoir to life. Through deep listening, careful narrative construction, and ethical storytelling, he helped translate lived experience into a voice that honors truth, vulnerability, and hope.

www.ingramcontent.com/pod-product-compliance
Lightning Source LLC
LaVergne TN
LVHW010945110826
845149LV00013B/2756

* 9 7 9 8 9 9 4 0 6 8 8 3 0 *